Typhoon IA/B
Combat Log

Operation Jubilee

August 1942

Hugh Harkins

Typhoon IA/B
Combat Log

© Hugh Harkins 2014

Published by Centurion Publishing
Glasgow
United Kingdom

ISBN 10: 1-903630-48-7
ISBN 13: 978-1-903630-48-8

This volume first published in 2014

Cover design © Centurion Publishing & Createspace

Page layout, concept and design © Centurion Publishing

The Publishers and Author would like to thank all organisations and services for their assistance and contributions in the preparation of this publication

CONTENTS

INTRODUCTION

The aim of this volume is to provide a comprehensive detailed study of the operational sorties and combat operations of the RAF's Hawker Typhoon IA/B fighter aircraft operating with the Duxford Typhoon Wing, consisting of No.56, 266 and 609 Squadrons, during Operation Jubilee (the combined operations raid on Dieppe) on 19 August 1942. A brief history of the genesis and operational fielding of the Typhoon, deliveries of which commenced in 1941, with operations commencing in May 1942, is provided, as is the specification and brief destruction of the Luftwaffe aircraft that it would join combat with over Dieppe – the Focke Wulf FW.190 fighter and the Dornier Do.217 twin-engine bomber.

The volume is supported by a wealth of operational documentation including pilot Combat Reports, Squadron Narratives and Wing Intelligence Combat Reports. In some cases spelling of specific places or names may vary slightly as some documents are reproduced verbatim. At times some operational documentation conflict with others in regards to events and timings.

FIGHTER COMMANDS ROAD TO DIEPPE

Operation Jubilee, the Combined Operations Raid on the defended port of Dieppe on the French Channel Coast on 19 August 1942, remains, even in the21st Century, an operation shrouded in mystery as to its true objectives. The truth is the raid, for all its rights and wrongs, had differing objectives for each of the armed services, the intelligence services and the political leaders ultimately responsible for ordering its execution.

For the politicians in Whitehall, and the Prime Minister Winston Churchill in particular, the raid appeared necessary as a timely show of reality to Britain's new ally, the United States of America; a nation that Churchill had been trying to get to join the allied war effort throughout the second half of 1940 and through 1941. Now allied with Britain and the Soviet Union since Germany declared war on America in December 1941, the United States growing economic and military power; the latter although still merely a token force in the war against Germany in 1942, was set to dominate in the coming years. The Soviet Leader, Joseph Stalin, had found in US President Theodore Roosevelt a willing ear in his cries for a second front in Europe, the latter promising the Soviets as much during high level meetings earlier in early 1942. The problem with these promises was that the United States did not possess the military forces to provide more than a mere token force of assistance to such an enterprise, which, if launched in summer 1942 would be completely reliant on British forces. The British government, while of little doubt that Britain was on the ascendance on the Channel front, was in no doubt that Britain could not launch a second front alone with much chance of success. To do so would be to sacrifice the forces she had so ardently built up at home and deprive the Middle East of much needed reinforcements, which could ultimately lead to the loss of the entire Middle East region; all this, with little realistic chance of success in Europe considering the few tens of Divisions that could be provided.

The Dieppe raid would show that an assault on a defended port was intimately doomed to failure, as the operation could not be conducted quickly or without extremely high casualties. The raid itself was limited to the time the objective was to be held; several hours at most. In the aftermath of the raid, Allied attention would turn to Operation Torch, the Anglo-US landings in French North Africa on 8 November 1942; Churchill had successfully won the argument that the Western Allies should first concentrate on the Mediterranean Theatre, an area which he of course had much political interest.

For the intelligence communities the combined operation at Dieppe was a chance to try and capture sensitive German documents, an operation which met with some success. For the Royal Navy, it showed the service was capable of operating off the enemy held coastline during daylight hours if required, albeit only if protected by a large defensive fighter force. For the RAF and Fighter Command in particular, it appeared to be a way to get the Luftwaffe to fight en-mass, by providing a major target which would have to be attacked. This, it was hoped, and even expected, would lead to the sure destruction of much of the Luftwaffe bomber and fighter forces on the Northern Channel front.

Since late 1940, Fighter Command, supported by the light bombers of No.2 Group Bomber Command, had conducted offensive sweeps over the Northern France and the Low Countries. These operations known as Rhubarbs and Circuses had varied in intensity. While the official position, based on combat claims, was that Fighter Command was coming off best in this battle of attrition. In reality the Luftwaffe was losing far fewer aircraft than Fighter Command. In March 1942 the RAF commenced a full scale offensive against the occupied territories across the English Channel, utilising the fighters of Fighter Command and Light Bombers of Bomber Command. The aim was to try and inflict heavy attrition on Luftwaffe fighter defenses by tying down Luftwaffe units on the Channel front.

During the four months of the main offensive, March until the end of June 1942, some 180 sorties a day were flown by Fighter Command sweeps, called 'Circus's', over France and Belgium, equating to more than 22,000 sorties. During this period Fighter Command lost more than 300 fighters on the offensive sweeps. As well as the Fighter Sweeps Bristol Blenheim and Douglas Boston III light bombers from No.2 Group Bomber Command were flown on raids across the Channel, around 700 sorties being flown during the March to June inclusive period, during the course of which 11 aircraft were lost. While it was hoped to inflict damage to ground installations such as airfields, the real role of the bombers was to entice German fighters to come up to intercept, where they could then be attacked by the RAF fighters.

Even with the heavy losses suffered by Fighter Command during the March-end of June offensive, it was being implied by some and inferred by others that Fighter Command was at least shooting down two enemy aircraft for every fighter it lost. There were some, however, who were slowly realising that at best this was not the case and at worse it may be the enemy who was shooting down two aircraft for everyone he lost. The reality was, of course, much worse, with

Fighter Command losing around 3 fighters for every German aircraft it destroyed during the air battles of the March – the end of June offensive. Fighter Command claimed more than 200 German fighters, mostly FW.190's, however, to the RAF's dismay; records later showed that the Luftwaffe lost only around 90 or so fighters. This showed what some in RAF intelligence already knew, or at least suspected, that the attrition of fighters on the Channel front was markedly in favour of the Germans, even more so than it had been during the battles of 1941. The only consolation that could be taken from these findings was that Britain could more easily replace its lost aircraft than could the Germans who were heavily committed in the war in the East against the Soviet Union.

There were a number of reasons for the Germans success against Fighter Command, not least of which was that the Luftwaffe's Focke Wulf FW.190, introduced in August 1941, was superior to the Supermarine Spitfire Vb, which was the best single-seat fighter in Fighter Command in late 1941 and the first half of 1942.

Such was the ascendancy of the FW.190 over the Spitfire Vb, that the new Hawker Typhoon IA/B fighters, which had come through a lengthy gestation to emerge as a high speed low-medium altitude bomber destroyer, would be wrongly employed on fighter sweeps while the RAF waited for its true counter to the FW.190 in the shape of the Spitfire IX and Spitfire VIII to enter service in numbers. While the Typhoon had performance attributes that made it a match for the FW.190 at lower altitudes, particularly in regards to speed, it lacked the performance at higher altitudes to compete with the FW.190 on equal terms; being particularly inferior in regards to maneuverability.

The FW.190's superiority over the Spitfire V would see Fighter Command call on the three Typhoon Squadrons of the Duxford Wing for the Dieppe operation as only four of the 48 Squadrons of Spitfires allocated to the operation were equipped with the new Spitfire IX's, some of which had only been operating the type for a few weeks.

11 Group Fighter Command, under Air Vice-Marshal Leigh-Mallory was entrusted to oversee control of the air protection portion of Operation Jubilee. A total of 56 single-engine fighter squadrons were allocated to the operation; 3 Hawker Typhoon IA/B, 5 Hawker Hurricane IIB/E, 4 Spitfire IX, 2 Spitfire VI and the balance being Spitfire V. In addition nine other squadrons would be allocated to the operation including 4 Squadrons of Mustangs from Army Co-Operation Command and 5 Squadrons of Boston and Blenheim light bombers from No.2 Group Bomber Command. There were a few other units also involved including 24 USAAF (United States Army Air Force) Boeing B-17 Flying Fortress four-engine bombers, tasked with a diversionary attack on Abbeville airfield, and 9 Boulton Paul Defiant calibration aircraft which were tasked with flying a feint towards Ostend in the hope that they would replicate a

large formation of bombers. In addition there were air sea rescue units available.

The composition of the air forces supporting the operation were overwhelmingly aimed at protecting the landings and shipping from interference from aircraft rather than actually providing support to ground forces by attacking strongpoint's. This would be a lesson that would be learned well when the allied armies landed at Normandy some 22 months later. However, for the Dieppe operation ground support was entrusted mainly to the handful of Hurricane, Blenheim and Boston squadrons.

When the days' fighting was over Fighter Command could take satisfaction that it had successfully protected the landing operation and naval convoys in the Channel, but at the cost of 98 aircraft lost and many more damaged. Other British air losses during the operation took the total to 106 (some operation documentation puts the figure at 108 and at least one document submitted to the Prime Minister stated 113; this latter document listing 98 from Fighter Command, 3 Boston from Bomber Command and 12 aircraft from Army-Cooperation Command). Fighter Commands "conservative estimate" of German losses in the air were put at 91 destroyed, 44 probably destroyed and 151 damaged. To many it seemed that Fighter Command had achieved its long-term goal of smashing the Luftwaffe fighter force in the west in a single running air battle lasting throughout the day. To this was added intelligence reports emanating from the Continent that "no less than 170" German aircraft had been destroyed in the days fighting. Over time, however, it started to become clear that German loses were nowhere near as high as had been estimated and post war German records confirmed that only 48 aircraft were destroyed with another 24 damaged. There was no doubt that the Luftwaffe had inflicted a higher level of attrition on the Allied Squadrons than they themselves had suffered. On a positive note for the RAF was the fact that the newer fighters such as the Typhoon and the Spitfire IX, the latter developed as the RAF's main counter to the superiority of the FW.190 over the Spitfire V, had fared well, inflicting higher losses than they themselves suffered at the hands of the Luftwaffe.

The RAF, including the three US Spitfire V Squadrons flew 2,366 sorties in support of the Dieppe operation. The high attrition the Spitfire Squadrons had suffered came mostly from those units operating the Spitfire V, not surprisingly as this variant made up the bulk of the Fighter Command assets employed in the operation. In the days following the operation 68 pilots of Fighter Command were reported missing from the 98 aircraft reported lost.

The Despatch submitted by the Naval Force Commander, Captain J. Hughes-Hallet R.N., to the Commander in Chief at Portsmouth Combined Headquarters, Fort Southwick, stated "The fighter cover afforded by No.11 Group was magnificent and the fact that a number of bombers got through was to be expected. It is considered that the loss of only one ship from bombing should be regarded as an unusually fortunate result."

4

2

OPERATION JUBILEE – AN OVERVIEW

Operation Jubilee was a Combined Operation involving significant air, naval and land forces. 11 Group Fighter Command under Air Vice-Marshal Leigh-Mallory had control of the air forces supporting the operation. He, along with the Naval Force Commander, Captain J. Hughes-Hallet R.N and the Military Force Commander, Major-General J.H. Roberts, reported to the Commander in Chief at Portsmouth Combined Headquarters, Fort Southwick.

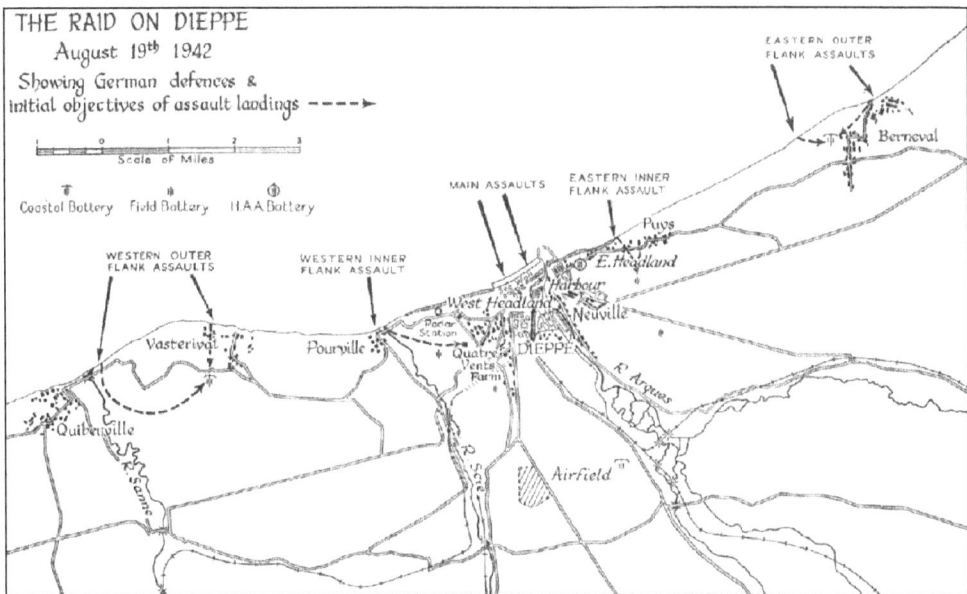

THE RAID ON DIEPPE
August 19th 1942
Showing German defences &
initial objectives of assault landings ----►

An overview of the official report on the operation is quoted below:

"A combined operation was carried out against Dieppe at dawn on the 19th August. The object of this operation was the destruction of local defences, power stations, aerodrome installations near the town and the capture and removal or destruction of German invasion barges and other craft. Although strategical surprise was impossible, tactical surprise was achieved, and the synchronisation of each part of the assault was perfect. The Force Commanders agreed that the inter-service co-operation throughout was of a very high standard.

The force to be landed consisted mainly of Canadians, but included Special Service troops, Royal Marines, a detachment from the United States Ranger battalion and a small contingent of Fighting French.

The crossing was successful except for a chance encounter by part of the flotilla with enemy flak ships and E-Boats. Our craft dispersed, and in the ensuing battle one flak ship was sunk and another damaged; the flotilla then reformed. Minesweeping was successfully carried out, and H.M. Destroyer *Calpe* (Force Commander's H.Q.s. ship) led the force through the minefield. The Dieppe harbor light remained on until our forces had got quite close. The destroyers carried out a preliminary bombardment quite successfully, but found that coastal artillery was a good deal stronger than had been anticipated. Simultaneously, Bostons and Hurricanes attacked coastal batteries and beaches, the main effort being diverted against five heavy gun positions, one of which appeared to have been put out of action. Smoke-screens were laid by some of the Bostons. Our fighters maintained a standing patrol of six squadrons over the target area up to 0620, when it was reduced to three squadrons.

Landings were made on six beaches. One flank attack by 265 men was very successfully carried out and a 6-in gun battery was completely put out of action, 160 Germans killed and four taken prisoner. The other flank attack, the scale of which was reduced by half through the chance encounter with E-boats previously mentioned, succeeded in interfering with the coastal battery on this front, but did not destroy it. These two successful actions enabled our ships to operate off Dieppe for the whole of the nine hours. Of the four landings in the centre, the first was successful and the Canadians fought their way inland, and although the second landing was successful, the Canadians were held up by very fierce opposition. On the other two beaches the opposition was again very fierce, but 18 tanks were got ashore. Great difficulty was experienced in the necessary demolition of the sea wall to enable tanks to get through, and, although some of them were able to operate most of the day round the Casino grounds, strong tank obstructions prevented them breaking into the town. A radio location station was destroyed.

Enemy air reaction started slowly but by 1000, over 80 enemy aircraft, including a number of bombers escorted by F.W. 190's were over the target area to attack our shipping, and the fighter cover was accordingly increased to 6 squadrons, which was maintained until 1645.

From 1000 onwards it was clear that the operation would not succeed, and the commanders decided not to land the remainder of the tanks. Embarkation commenced at 1106. From 1200 onwards enemy bombers continued to attack, but were unescorted apart from the general fighter cover which the enemy was maintaining.

By 1215 the situation on the beaches was grave and orders were given to blow up the tanks, which had met with considerable artillery fire. By 1410 the last ship of the force was three miles clear on the return journey, and the force arrived in harbor without further interference, covered by our fighters. Fifty German prisoners were brought back.

Of the Naval force taking part, H.M Destroyer *Berkeley* was damaged by bombing and subsequently sunk. H.M. Destroyers *Calpe*, *Brocklesby*, the Polish destroyer *Slazak* and a steam gun-boat were damaged. 42 landing craft were sunk or missing out of a total of 167. Naval casualties were 100 missing.

Of the 6,000 soldiers taking part about one-third are missing, and of these the Germans claim 1,500 prisoners.

Air support to the operation was supplied by about 56 fighter squadrons, including three United States Squadrons (involving a total of 2,366 sorties), six Army Co-operation squadrons, three Bomber Command squadrons and 24 United States Fortresses. In the heavy air fighting which took place took place, 93 enemy aircraft were destroyed, 39 were probably destroyed and 140 were damaged. Included in these casualties were 149 F.W. 190's and more than 100 bombers. Our losses were 98 aircraft of Fighter Command (68 pilots are missing), 12 Army Co-operation Command aircraft and three Bostons of Bomber Command."

Top: The Royal Navy Destroyer HMS *Berkeley*, the only major naval casualty of the operation, settling in the water severely damaged after being bombed by a German bomber. The vessel was later sunk by a British torpedo. Above: A Boston III from 88 Squadron passes into France following a bombing attack on the coast defence batteries at Dieppe; upper left of photograph. RAF

3

DUXFORD WING TYPHOON OPERATIONS – OPERATION JUBILEE

By 19 August 1942, when the Typhoon was committed to the large scale Combined Operation over Dieppe, the aircraft was to all intents and purposes untried, having entered operational service only in the few moths preceding the Dieppe raid. In those few months it had flown a variety of missions ranging from interception of enemy reconnaissance aircraft to fighter sweeps over the Continent, shooting down two Junkers Ju.88's in the former role. However, although there had been a few encounters with the Luftwaffe's FW.190 fighters, combat proper had not been joined.

Duxford had been selected for the formation of what became known as the Duxford Typhoon Wing for a number of reasons, not least being that it was in a quite sector. No. 56 Squadron was selected to be the first Squadron to convert to the Typhoon, commencing replacement of its Hawker Hurricanes with the Typhoon IA in September 1941. No.266 (Rhodesia) Squadron began conversion to Typhoons in January 1942, relinquishing its last operational Spitfire in May that year. The third Squadron of what would become known as the Duxford Typhoon Wing, No. 609 (West Riding) Squadron, began conversion to the Typhoon in April 1942 and was ready to commence operation on this type by 30 June that year.

Although the Typhoon was still suffering a number of problems, structural and with the Napier Sabre piston engine, by early summer 1942 confidence in the aircraft was high enough for the aircraft to enter operational service, two Squadrons, 56 and 266, being declared operational in May and the third, 609, at the end of June.

Once operational, the Typhoon Squadrons took on "normal sector duties", including scrambles to intercept suspected bogeys (39 being conducted over the next few months). The Typhoon wing was allocated a number of roles, some of which the Typhoon was suitable for, some for which it was ideal and others that it was simply not suitable for. The role most suitable for the aircraft was the "Special Anti-Recco" patrols", 29 of which were flown off the Norfolk coast over the next few months. These patrols were distinct from the "Special anti-fighter bomber patrols", a number of which were flown from RAF Manston and Tangmere. The Wing also flew convoy protection patrols and escort patrols for High Speed Launch's searching for downed aircrew among other duties

The type of mission most likely to bring the Typhoon into contact with the FW.190 was the medium altitude anti-fighter sweeps carried out along the Continental coastline between Ostend and Dieppe. These sweeps, 19 of which were flown over the summer months and beyond the Dieppe raid, would cross the coast penetrating as far as St. Omar and Hesdin.

No.56 Squadron was the first Squadron to convert to the Typhoon, receiving its first examples in September 1941. The Squadron was declared operational with a mix of Typhoon IA and IB fighters in May 1942. This formation of 56 Squadron Typhoons is seen post Operation Jubilee. RAF

On 9 August 1942, 12 Typhoons from 266 Squadron, 6 from 56 Squadron and 3 from 609 Squadron, practiced interceptions of 9 Boeing B-17 Flying Fortress bombers at 26,000 feet, which were escorted by Spitfires at 28,000 feet. This exercise proved beyond doubt that the Typhoon was at a major disadvantage against dedicated fighter aircraft at higher altitudes. The official consensus was that "The height was too great for the Typhoons to operate well and the advantage was with the Spitfires."

In general it was considered that on average the pilots of the Duxford Typhoon wing were "considerably more experienced than those of the average Spitfire Squadron". Some had flown Spitfires on fighter sweeps during the 1941 campaigns, when such sweeps were deep penetrations, rather than grazing enemy occupied territory as much of the summer 1942 sweeps were designed to do for reasons of economy. S/Ldr. Richey of 609 Squadron for instance had flown some 50 such sweeps. Even so, it was reported by S/Ldr. Richey that "… many of the Typhoon pilots, especially those with operational experience, feel a very definite sense of inferiority as regards fighting the F.W.190 on its own terms." His report, prepared after the Dieppe operation, went on to state "This is not unnatural, for the Typhoon was not designed primarily for fighting fighters, whereas the F.W 190 obviously was."

Prior to the Dieppe operation on 19 August, results achieved by the Wing were on the whole considered to be poor. The Fighter Roadsteads and fighter sweeps had produced no results, nor had the anti-fighter bomber patrols. While official documentation states nothing achieved in the Convoy patrols and escorts for High Speed Launches, this is misleading as the intention was merely to protect the surface vessels, a role which was accomplished. The most profitable missions were the special anti-recco patrols, which resulted in 2 Junkers Ju.88's being shot down, an Air Ministry report stating that they "were easily overtaken and shot down'".

In the first confirmed victory for the Typhoon Wing, Typhoons, R7822 (P/O Munro) and R7696 (P/O Lucas), from No.266 Squadron took off at 19.25 hours on a sea patrol during which they encountered a Ju.88 approaching from the 2 O'clock position at "0 feet" altitude. Red 1 was flying at 800 feet, with Red 2 ant 50, Munro turning to port and Lucas turning to starboard to pursue the Ju.88 in a stern chase. With Munro positioned "dead astern" and Lucas slightly offset to port, the Ju.88 opened fire at a range of between 800 to 1,000 yards, while starting a weave to port, which now brought Lucas into position dead astern, prompting the Ju.88 to return to his original course, apparently increasing speed as black smoke appeared indicating full boost was used. The two Typhoons were fast reducing the range to between 400 and 600 yards when Munro fired a short burst of 20 mm cannon, observing strikes go into the water. Munro then throttled back to +2 Boost, reducing the range to 200 yards when a 3 second burst was fired. Around this time Lucas also opened fire with a short burst from the port quarter at a range of 600 yards, followed by a further short burst at 400 yards and a long burst at 200 yards. With both pilots firing, flames appeared from the Ju.88 inboard of both engine nacelles. A "hood" was noted to have come off and one of the Ju.88 crew apparently started to climb out, but then slumped back, probably hit as the Typhoons were still firing. The Ju.88 then "bounced on the sea, dropped a wing and went straight in", no survivors being found.

Here taking off later in 1942, Typhoon IA, R7648 was one of the Typhoons operating with the Duxford Typhoon Wing over Dieppe on 19 August 1942. RAF

This shared kill for Munro and Lucas was the first air combat victory credited to Typhoons. Another Ju.88 was shot down under similar circumstances by F/Lt. Johnston of 266 Squadron flying Typhoon R7819 on an evening sea patrol in company with three other Typhoons on 13 August.

Prior to the Dieppe raid the Duxford Wings operations had resulted in the loss of three Typhoons on operational sorties; all shot down by Spitfires, apparently mistaking the Typhoons for enemy FW.190's.

On 17 August, two days before the Dieppe raid, the Duxford Wing, 12 Typhoons from 266 Squadron, 11 from 609 Squadron and 8 from 56 Squadron, was on a fighter Sweep of Griz Nez, Dunkirk, Nieuport. Control informed of FW.190's in the area, but only 56 Squadron sighted any, although no combats took place. These early operations were conducted using a mix of Typhoon IA and IB fighters and both models would be employed during the Dieppe operation on 19 August.

The first operational sorties in support of operational Jubilee for the Duxford Typhoon Wing were flown much later than many of the other Squadrons involved in the operation. The lead Squadron of the Wing, 609, took off from Duxford at 10.55 on the morning of 19 August 1942, followed by 266 and 56 Squadrons which took off from Duxford at 11.00.

The aircraft and pilots for the respective Squadrons were as follows:

609 Squadron - Took off at 10.55 and landed at 12.15 except R7961, which landed at 11.15.

Aircraft	Pilot
R7961	F/O R.E.J. Wilmet
R7677	F/Lt. J.A. Atkinson
R7752	S/Ldr. P.H.M. Richey
R7681	P/O R. Dopere
R7845	Sgt. A.C de Saxce
R7690	P/O C.C Ortmans
R7680	P/O G. Evans
R7708	F/Lt. R.F. Beamont
R7849	F/O J.C. Wells
R7595	P/O R.J. Roelandt
R8221	Sgt. A.R. Blanco

266 Squadron - Took off at 11.00 and landed at 12.10 except R7627 (spare), which landed at 11.45.

Aircraft	Pilot
R7686	S/Ldr. C.L. Green
R7814	P/O N.J. Lucas
R7815	F/Lt. R.H.L. Dawson
R7813	P/O W.S. Smithyman
R7822	P/O I.M. Munro
R7645	P/O J.D. Wright
R7698	W/Cdr. D.E. Gillam
R7819	F/Lt. A.C. Johnston
R7672	P/O J.D. Miller
R7715	P/O J.C Thomson
R7821	P/O W.J.A Wilson
R7687	P/O G. Elcombe
R7649	Sgt. J. Harwith
R7627	P/O J.H. Deal (Spare)

56 Squadron - Took off at 11.00 and landed at 12.20.

Aircraft   **Pilot**

R7825   S/Ldr. Dundas H.S.L.
R7854   Sgt. Stimpson C.T.
R8200   P/O Dring W.
R7633   F/Sgt. Mouat W.I.
R7739   P/O Piltingsrud G.
R7679   F/Lt. Ingle-finch M.R
R7702   P/O Reed J.L
R7711   P/O Haabjoern E.
R7652   P/O Coombes W.E.
R7846   P/O Macdonald K.F.
R7648   P/O Doniger N.A.

Once airborne the Typhoon Wing headed for a rendezvous with 9 Boulton Paul Defiant calibration aircraft which had taken off from Clackton. The Defiants were to fly to an area about 10 miles out from Ostend, with the aim of giving the impression of a major raid in that direction, thus distracting some of the German defensive attention from the ongoing Dieppe operation. The Wing, flying at 18,000 feet, was out ahead of the Defiants with the aim of attacking German fighters sent up to attack the decoy raid. The Typhoons continued until near Ostend then turned and swept down the coast towards Mardych, but no German aircraft or anti-aircraft fire were encountered. The Typhoons returned, but landed at West Malling between 12.10 and 12.20 due to fuel shortages.

No.609 Squadron Narrative – 1st sweep:

"The alarums and discursions of the night before, and the tense air of secrecy, have formed the impression on most pilots' minds that today they will be called on either to assist or to repel an invasion – more probably the former. This impression is confirmed when at a short briefing about 0900 the W/C refers them to the 8 O'Clock news mentioning Combined Operations. Still without knowing anything about the operation as a whole (except that it is called 'JUBILEE') 12 aircraft led by W/C Gillam set out at 1053 as a leading squadron of the Typhoon wing to rendezvous at Orfordness on the Suffolk coast with 9 special calibration Defiants. Escorting these from 18000 ft they fly up the enemy coastline from Mardyck to Ostend and... well that is all: they have fulfilled their mission of trying to distract attention from Dieppe. Landing at West Malling at 1215 (except the C.O., who has had to return to Duxford to change his aircraft)..."

No.266 Squadron Narrative – 1st sweep:

"In the night and very early morning the combined operational landing at Dieppe took place and the land fighting continued there most of the day. This squadron went on three wing sweeps with 609 and 56. The first in the morning was a diversionary attack. Our wing was to protect 9 Defiants which were arranged to look like a large bomber force attacking east of Calais. No E/A were seen and the sweep was quite uneventful except that everybody was short of petrol and had to land at West Malling."

2nd Sweep – 14.00-13.15

The three Squadrons of the Wing took off at 14.00 hours with orders to sweep the area Le Touquet – Le Treport to protect the vessels involved in Operation Jubilee. The Squadrons were arranged with 609 leading, then 266 and 56 Squadron providing top cover. The aircraft and pilots for the respective Squadrons were as follows:

609 Squadron - Took off at 14.00 and landed between 15.05 and 15.15.

Aircraft	Pilot
R7961	F/O R.E.J. Wilmet
R7708	F/Lt. R.F. Beamont
R7849	F/O J.C. Wells
R7595	P/O R.J. Roelandt
R8221	S/Ldr. F.H.M. Richey
R7713	Sgt. A.R. Blanco
R7677	F/Lt. J.A. Atkinson
R7690	P/O C.C Ortmans (returned to base at 14.10)
R7845	Sgt. A.C de Saxce
R7680	P/O G. Evans
R7681	P/O R. Dopere

266 Squadron - Took off at 14.00 and landed at 15.05.

Aircraft	Pilot
R7686	S/Ldr. C.L. Green
R7814	P/O N.J. Lucas
R7815	F/Lt. R.H.L. Dawson
R7813	P/O W.S. Smithyman
R7822	P/O I.M. Munro
R7645	P/O J.D. Wright (failed to get airborne)
R7698	W/Cdr. D.E. Gillam
R7819	F/Lt. A.C. Johnston
R7672	P/O J.D. Miller
R7715	P/O J.C Thomson
R7821	P/O W.J.A Wilson
R7687	P/O G. Elcombe

56 Squadron - Took off between 14.00 and 14.30 and landed between 15.00 and 15.40.

Aircraft	Pilot
R7714	S/Ldr. Dundas H.S.L.
R7854	Sgt. Stimpson C.T.
R8200	P/O Dring W.
R7633	F/Sgt. Mouat W.I.
R7739	P/O Piltingsrud G.
R7714	F/O Poulter V.G
R7679	F/Lt. Ingle-finch M.R.
R7202	P/O Reed J.L.
R7711	P/O Haabjoern E.
R7652	P/O Coombes W.E.
R7846	P/O Macdonald K.F.
R7648	P/O Doniger N.A.

Note: R7414 is listed in Squadron operational records twice for this mission, each time with different pilots; S/Ldr. Dundas and P/O Poulter.

No.609 Squadron Narrative – 2nd sweep

"... they take off again at 1400 hours with orders to sweep from Le Touquet to Le Treport. Order of Battle:-

Yellow	Red	Blue
F/Lt. Atkinson	W/C Gillam	F/Lt. Beamont
P/O Dopere	P/O Evans	P/O Wells
F/O Wilmet	S/L Richey	P/O Rolandt
Sgt. De Saxce	P/O Ortmans	Sgt. Blanco

... but P/O Ortmans fails to start his aircraft. 609 is again leading at 15000 ft when bombers are reported approaching our ships off Dieppe from the direction of Merville. These (3 Dornier's) are duly sighted and attacked with success by 266. About 20 Fw 190's are then sighted in loose formation, 5000 ft below and 5 miles inland, headed north. Unfortunately the W/C does not see them for some time, but finally leads 609 towards 4 one mile to port, 609 now being at about the same level. On sighting the Typhoons, the 190's turn to port and begin a steep dive through cloud. 609 give chase and only break off the dive on emerging below cloud at 10000 ft, by which time the W/C has decreased his own range to about 400 yds, and takes a squirt. The only pilot of 609 to fire is Sgt. De Saxce. During the dive he has seen the strange sight of a 190 formating line abreast of F/O Wilmet, but his French is not understood by the Belgian. When Wilmet and his new pal pull out, de Saxce takes a short squirt at the latter from 100 yards beam, but sees no result. Most 609 aircraft then recross the coast west of Dieppe, P/O Dopere getting separated and becoming mildly involved with 1 or 2 190's before coming back and landing, not at West Malling, but at Duxford – because, as he tells the station I.O., he wants to go on leave before dark. He also reports that he and de Saxce have seen some He 111's on an aerodrome thought to be St Valery en Caux. F/O Wilmet continues his adventures by also losing the squadron and steering north at 0 ft, weaving and looking for an inland target. S.E. of Le Touquet he passes a 190 head on, and emerging from France in that area, sees a whole lot of little ships with the French flag painted on the side. Finally, on the way to Dungeness, he gets shot at by a Spit IX, fortunately with insufficient deflection. All 609 (except Dopere) land intact at W. Malling by 1515, but 266 have lost F/Lt. Dawson and another pilot, probably both to Spitfires, who if so can now claim 5 Typhoons to the Germans nil. A Dornier destroyed is claimed for Dawson, and other claims for 266 are 1 Dornier and 1 Fw 190 probable."

Note: Only F/Lt. Dawson was shot down by Spitfires, the best evidence being that the other Typhoon was shot down by a FW.190 or defensive fire from a Dornier Do.217.

"Wing led by W/Cmdr GILLAM, DSO, DFC & Bar, AFC. Took off from West Malling (P/O WRIGHT did not get his aircraft of the ground) 609 Squadron leading 266 and 56 Squadrons top. Wing flew to Le TREPORT and were warned by control of Enemy Bombers. Some of our Squadron at 16,000 feet saw three Dorniers inland of Le TREPORT with several FW.190 in the vicinity and reported. Yellow section F/Lt. DAWSON and P/O SMITHYMAN and White 1 P/O. MUNRO, were ordered by F/Lt. DAWSON to attack the Dorniers. From what Pilots heard on the R/T it appears that P/O SMITHYMAN saw one Dornier crashing and that F/Lt. DAWSON said that it was his. P/O. MUNRO diving fast fired one burst (100 Cannon) from 300 closing to 50 yards and saw smoke issuing from the Dornier between the Port Engine and the fuselage, as the Dornier dived steeply down. Claiming one Do.217 probably destroyed. He had to break away and noticed tracer going past his wings. He went down to 0 feet and on coming out over coast saw a Typhoon and found that it was F/Lt. DAWSON. F/Lt. JOHNSTON, Blue 1 with his No.2 and Green 1, when at 15,000 ft. just N. of Le TREPORT saw ten FW.190 below at 2 o'clock. F/Lt. JOHNSTON Dived after them, 8 breaking away to port and two dived straight ahead. Following one of these two F/Lt. JOHNSTON using full throttle caught up and fired a short burst at 600 yds range and series of short bursts as range closed to 400 yds. E/A steepened his dive to nearly vertical and F/Lt. JOHNSTON and Blue 2, P/O. MILLER saw thick white smoke issuing from the FW.190. F/Lt. JOHNSTON had to pull out on account of his speed (480 m.p.h.) and low ground haze. He claims one FW.190 probably destroyed. F/Lt. DAWSON and P/O MUNRO flew in line abreast over the CHANNEL and got near to Blue and Green Sections. About half way over the CHANNEL a Squadron of Spitfires came in on the Starboard quarter. All our aircraft at once used full boost to get away, some weaved but one Spitfire opened fire on F/Lt. DAWSON aircraft. P/O. MUNRO saw pieces fly off and DAWSON's aircraft half rolled up to 100 feet and then went straight into the sea. There was no sign of the wreckage or pilot. Red and Black sections came home at 14,000 feet and they too complained that Spitfires attacked them although they did not actually open fire. P/O SMITHYMAN is missing no one saw him after they started to attack the three Dorniers. Rest of Squadron landed at West Malling."

No.266 Squadron 2nd Narrative – 2st sweep **"The second sweep was from West Malling down to the battle area near Dieppe. F/Lt. Dawson, P/O. Smithyman and P/O Munro saw and attacked 3 Do.217 and it is believed that F/Lt. Dawson destroyed one also P/O. Munro claims one probably destroyed. There were some F.W.190's in the vicinity and P/O Munro saw tracer going past his wing at the end of the combat. P/O. Smithyman is missing. From R/T interceptions several pilots understand that F/Lt. Dawson destroyed one. F/Lt. Johnston dived after 10 F.W.190's and probably destroyed one in a dive from 15000 feet to near the deck at 480 m.p.h. P/O Munro and F/Lt. Dawson returning home at 0 feet when half way over the channel suddenly met a Squadron of Spitfires all of which looked as if they were attacking; one of which fired at F/Lt. Dawson whose A/C went straight into the sea. S/Ldr. Green with three others came out from the French coast at 14000 feet and they also complain that 4 Spitfires flew at them in a very menacing manner but fortunately did not open fire. Results of the day 1 Dornier 217 destroyed by F/Lt. Dawson 1 Dornier 217 probably destroyed by P/O. Munro, 1 F.W.190 probably destroyed by F/Lt. Johnston. Our losses P/O Smithyman missing. And F/Lt. Dawson missing believed killed…"**

56 Squadron Narrative of the 2nd Sweep – 14.00 to 15.15

"A second sortie started from West Malling at 14.00 hours. The Squadron were top cover squadron with No.266 below and 609 bottom at 15000 feet. Our instructions were to go down to Le Treport and sweep to Le Touquet. When about ten miles from the coast Control reported some bombers coming from Douai to attack home bound shipping. The wing turned to starboard and at the coast 266 and 609 squadrons had a mix up with three Dornier 217 and eight to twelve F.W.190's. No.56 Squadron was left at 17000 feet as top cover, owing to the presence of several enemy fighters at superior altitudes. The squadron maintained its position above the other two while they were attacking, and for several minutes diving attacks by F.W.190's were held off by steep turning counter attacks. These attacks were made by small numbers of enemy aircraft diving out of the sun, except in the last case when a force of eight to twelve dived from about 5000 feet above; the lower two squadrons had by then withdrawn, so the Squadron Leader gave the order to dive away to the North, owing to the enemy's superior tactical position.
The whole squadron landed at West Malling and although no casualties were inflicted on the enemy, the sky was kept clear above the other two squadrons, and it was proved for the first time that Typhoons can compete with and outpace the F.W.190 at medium altitudes, even though it cannot out manoeuvre."

No.12 Group: 28/8/42.   Copy to Fighter Command.

INTELLIGENCE FORM "F".

Claim on behalf of F/Lt. Dawson (Rhodesian).

A. 19.8.42.   F. Fine, Visibility good.
B. No.266 (Rhodesian) Sqdn.   G. 1 Typhoon missing.

C. Typhoon IB.   H. F/Lt. Dawson (Rhodesian)
                                     Missing believed killed.

E. Between Le Treport & Dieppe   J. 1 Do.217 destroyed.

                                     K. ---

Further to composite Combat Report and to Intelligence Form "F" for the second Typhoon Wing sortie of August 19th, Operation Jubilee.

F/Lt. Dawson, Yellow I, and P/O. Smithyman, Yellow II, with P/O. Munro, White I, (White II never got airborne at take off) were flying together and went in to attack three Do.217's on F/Lt. Dawson's order. P/O. Munro arranged for F/Lt. Dawson to take the starboard one, while he took the port one.

P/O. Munro after the engagement, by chance met F/Lt. Dawson coming out of French Coast and flew with him towards England, but they were suddenly attacked by some Spitfires and F/Lt. Dawson's aircraft was seen to be hit and to go into the sea. He is missing; so also is his No.2 P/O Smithyman, who was not seen by anyone after the beginning of the attack on the 3 Dorniers.

The following R/T messages were heard.

S/L. GREEN heard: A. "Theres one just gone in."
                     B. (Dawson's voice) "Yes, it's mine."
                     A. "I have just damaged one."
                     B. "(Dawson's voice) "That makes two."
P/O. MUNRO heard: A. "There's one gone in."
                     B. "I think it's mine." (Dawson's voice)

P/O. THOMSON " A. "Is that yours going in?"
                 B. "Yes, it's mine."
P/O. WILSON   " A. "Is that yours going in Rollo?"
                 (Rollo is F/Lt. Dawson's Christian name)
                 B. "Yes, that's mine."

There is no record of any such R/T messages on the Hornchurch R/T log, but the action took place over Le Treport and the distance may have been excessive, and there was also a lot of other R/T talk at the time.

The height from which the transmissions were made is not known, but it is more than likely that, since it was after the engagements, our aircraft had come down to near zero feet.

(sgd)   illegible
Flying Officer
Intelligence Officer, 266 (Rhodesia) Sqdn.

(sgd)   **Green**
Squadron Leader
Officer Commanding, 266 (Rhodesia) Sqdn.

(sgd)   **Munro**
Pilot Officer
Pilot Officer, 266 (Rhodesia) Sqdn.

(sgd)   illegible
Pilot Officer
Pilot Officer, 266 (Rhodesia) Sqdn.

(sgd)   **Thomson**
Pilot Officer
Pilot Officer, 266 (Rhodesia) Sqdn.

Following the Sweep the Wing returned to West Malling with the exception of the two Typhoons of No.266 Squadron which were lost and one aircraft which returned to Duxford. 56 and 266 Squadrons are recorded as having landed at 15.00 and 609 Squadron is recorded as landing at 15.15.

Page 22: Cine Gun Camera footage of a Dornier Do.217 being shot down over the English Channel by a Spitfire V of 312 (Czech) Squadron, which was patrolling over shipping returning from the Dieppe raid. Page 23: a Do.217 is shot down by a Spitfire VB from 317 (Polish) Squadron over Dieppe. Above: Shown for illustration purposes, this Cine Gun Camera footage shows a FW.190 being shot down by A 266 Squadron Typhoon IB post Operation Jubilee. RAF

3rd Sweep – 16.50-18.20

The Wing was tasked with flying a third sweep; this time from the Somme Estuary to Griz Nez. 56 Squadron took off at 16.50, 266 Squadron took off at 17.00 and 609 Squadron took off between 17.00 and 17.10. The Wing Commander had to return to base due to an open gun mounting and eight of 609 Squadron turned and followed him home. The remainder of the Squadron continued with 56 and 266 Squadrons to complete the sweep, encountering no enemy aircraft or anti-aircraft fire.

266 Squadron

Aircraft	Pilot
R7686	S/Ldr. C.L. Green
R7814	P/O N.J. Lucas
R7822	P/O I.M. Munro
R7672	F/O F.B. Biddulph
R7698	W/Cdr. D.E. Gillam
R7819	F/Lt. A.C. Johnston
R7672	P/O J.D. Miller
R7715	P/O J.C Thomson
R7821	P/O W.J.A Wilson
R7687	P/O G. Elcombe
R7649	Sgt. J. Howarth
R7847	P/O J.H. Deall
R7589	P/O J. Small

Note: Typhoon R7672 is listed twice in form 541, each time with separate pilots; F/O Biddulph and P/O Miller respectively.

609 Squadron

Aircraft	Pilot
R7706	P/O Y.R.G. Creteur
R7681	Sgt. A.R. Blanco
R7677	F/Lt. J.A. Atkinson
R7690	P/O C.C Ortmans
R7845	Sgt. A.C de Saxce
R7680	P/O G. Evans

R7855	Sgt. A. Haddon
R7961	F/O R.E.J. Wilmet
R7708	F/Lt. R.F. Beamont
R7849	F/O J.C. Wells
R7595	P/O R.J. Roelandt
R8221	S/Ldr. F.H.M. Richey
R7713	F/O J.G. Astrbury

56 Squadron

Aircraft	Pilot
R7825	S/Ldr. Dundas H.S.L.
R7854	Sgt. Stimpson C.T
R8200	P/O Dring W.
R7633	F/Sgt. Mouat W.I.
R7739	P/O Piltingsrud G
R7714	F/O Poulter V.G.
R7679	F/Lt. Ingle-finch M.R
R7823	P/O Reed J.L
R7711	P/O Haabjoern E.
R7653	P/O Coombes W.E.
R7846	Sgt. Cueto F.
R7648	P/O Doniger N.A.

Note: Serial 7653 flown by P/O Coombes may be a misprint in the Squadron records that should possibly read R7652, which was the aircraft he flew on the previous two sorties.

266 Squadron Narrative of the 3rd sweep

"Took off from West Malling with W/Cdr Gillam DSO, DFC & BAR, APC, Leading but he had to return as his gun mounting had come open and eight of 609 Squadron being on the wrong button followed him. S/Ldr. Green then led. The wing crossed French coast just N. of SOMME at 12,000 feet and swept up just inside coast over BOULOGNE then on 340° out over GRIZ NEZ. Wing did not go inland to ST OMER as ordered as there was 10/10 cloud inland. Saw no E/A and no Flak. Squadron landed back at DUXFORD."

No.609 Squadron Narrative 3rd sweep

"At 1540 F/O Astbury and Sgt. Haddon are dispatched from Duxford as serviceable reinforcements, and are both rewarded by completing their first sweep – 2 of the few 609 aircraft which do. This time the order is to sweep from the Somme Estuary to Boulogne, and they take off at 1710. Unfortunately the C.O. again has trouble, and when the W/C suffers likewise and breaks away home, no less than 8 609 aircraft follow him. The rest, with 266 and 56 squadrons, complete the operation without opposition, and all land back at Duxford by 1820, feeling that the squadron has at last taken a little part in the war for a change."

No.56 Squadron Narrative of the 3rd sweep

"A third sortie was made from West Malling at 17.00 hours and lasted an hour. The Wing Leader had to return as his port gun panel had not been fastened down and through being on the wrong button eight of No.609 squadron followed him home. The remaining aircraft under the leadership of S/Ldr. Green of No.266 Squadron swept the coast from Le Touquet to Boulogne and then straight home."

Returning from the third sweep of the day the Wing returned and landed at Duxford. 56 Squadron landed at 18.05, 266 Squadron landed at 18.00, with the exception of R7698 (W/Cdr. Gillam) who landed at 17.50, and 609 landed at staggered times between 17.40 and 18.20.

This ended the Duxford Typhoon Wings participation in Operation Jubilee. 266 Squadron had flown 39 sorties during the 3 sweeps (includes a few air spares), 56 Squadron had flown 35 sorties and 609 Squadron had flown 35 sorties for a Wing total of 109 operational sorties. Of the two aircraft lost in the operation one was confirmed definitely shot down by a Spitfire, while the other was almost certainly shot down by enemy action. The most likely cause was the attack by FW.190's, although there is also the possibility that return fire from a Do.217 was responsible.

As well as the operational sorties over enemy territory all Squadrons flew a number of non-operational and operational transfer sorties of aircraft between Snailwell, Duxford and West Malling.

The following Intelligence report was submitted to Fighter Command following the Dieppe operation:

<u>SECRET</u>   <u>Appendix A</u>   <u>COPY</u>
                                                                                    110

<u>INTELLIGENCE – FORM "F</u>

<u>OPERATION "JUBILEE"</u>

A. 19th August 1942.   F. Good. Haze low down.
                                                                     5/10 cloud at 5,000 feet

B. Duxford Typhoon Wing.   G. 2 Typhoons Cat. E.

C. Typhoons 1A and 1B. 34 a/c.   H. 2 Pilots missing. F/Lt.
                                                                      Dawson & P/O Smithyman,
                                                                      266 Squadron

D. 1430 approx.

E. Near Dieppe   J. 1 Do.217 destroyed, 1
                                                                     Do.217 prob. 1 FW.190
                                                                     probably destroyed.

K. Nil

GENERAL.

     The Wing led by W/Cdr. D.E. Gillam, D.S.O., D.F.C. and bar, A.R.C., leading 609 Sqdn (bottom), 266 (Rhodesia) Sqdn (middle), and 56 Sqdn (top), took off on their second sortie of the day from West Malling at 1400 hours, 30 a/c landing there at 1510 hours. They were ordered to proceed to Le Treport and sweep up the coast to Le Touquet.

     When about 10 miles from Le Treport, Control informed Wing Leader that enemy bombers were making for our line of homebound shipping, so Wing turned to starboard. Wing was at 17,000 to 15,000 feet. Three Do.217's were reported and sighted near the Coast approaching our shipping from Merville direction in a tight vic. F/Lt. Dawson, P/O Smithyman and P/O Munro, 266 Sqn, attacked these. Someone was heard to say over the R/T "There one gone" and F/Lt. Dawson was heard to say "Yes, it's mine." P/O Munro also engaged and claims another as probably destroyed. As they attacked, 3 FW.190's attacked from above and P/O Smithyman was not seen again.

Then about 20 FW.190's were seen about 5,000 feet below on both sides of wing going North about 5 miles inland and 3 to 4,000 yards away. Wing Leader told 266 to take any target and led 609 Squadron after 5 of the enemy a/c. The enemy a/c half rolled back further inland, diving steeply and 609 followed at full boost decreasing range to 400 yards at 1,000 feet when they pulled out of the dive. Wing Leader fired a long burst at one of the 5 and, as he pulled out of his dive, he saw four enemy a/c fan out as they pulled out. But no sign of the one he fired at. Yellow 4 of 609 Sqdn. (Sgt. De Saxo-French) saw a FW.190 formating abreast of Yellow 3 during the dive and fired a short burst from the beam at 100 yards range but observed no results. Most of 609 Sqdn. Recrossed the coast West of Dieppe, but Yellow 3 (F/O. Wilmet – Belgian) lost them and turned North at zero feet, weaving and looking for a target. He passed one FW.190 head on S.E. of Le Touquet and crossing the coast there saw about 25 small ships with French flag on the hulls amidships. Most were sailing vessels, but some had funnels. As he made for Dungeness 2 a/c approached from port. He turned towards them and identified them as Spitfire IX's. No.2 of these fired at him. P/O Dopere (Yellow 2 – Belgian) and Sgt. De Saxce had also become separated from the Squadron and, flying over an aerodrome thought to be St Valery en Caux, saw several He.111's on the ground. They were fired on by some ground defences but were not hit and landed at Duxford and Hawkinge respectively.

As Wing Leader and 609 Sqdn. went in to attack, some of 266 Sqdn. Attacked some more FW.190's which, it is thought, sought to dive on 609 Sqdn. F/Lt. Johnston, 266 Sqdn, attacked one which he claims as probably destroyed for, after firing several short bursts, he saw it steepen its dive to nearly vertical. He saw no strikes but both he and P/O Miller of the same Sqdn. Saw white smoke pouring from it and when lasts seen it was going down vertically into the haze at 1,000 feet. It is though P/O. Smithyman was picked off by one of these FW.190's.

Returning home, Wing flew along the line of shipping at zero feet and saw a Squadron of Spitfires coming in on the starboard quarter in line astern. P/O. Munro (266 Sqdn) saw No.3 of the starboard section fire at F/Lt. Dawson. Pieces flew of his a/c and it slowly half rolled up to 100 feet and then went straight into the sea.

A Do.217 is claimed as destroyed by F/Lt. Dawson in view of the R/T conversation.

56 Squadron were not called down to assist and had no engagements.

Sgt. De Saxce fired 57 rounds of ball and 58 rounds H.E.I from cannons. No stoppages. He carried C.G.C. but it was not used.

No claim is made for Wing Leader but he exposed a cine film and, when this has been assessed, it may be possible to make one. He fired 180 rounds of cannon, 50 from each port gun and starboard outer and 30 from starboard inner.

(SGD)   E. Mitchell,
Flight Lieutenant,
Sector Intelligence Officer,
Duxford. Cambs.

Postscript

The Dieppe Operation and the few months of operations beforehand were just the beginning for the Typhoon. Once most of the structural and technical issues had been ironed out the aircraft was successfully employed in interceptions of the so called 'tip and run' fast raiders, FW.190 and Me.109's, conducting bombing attacks on the south east coast of England. Trials with bombs were conducted later in 1942 and the Typhoon IB and later IIB was successfully employed as a fighter bomber using cannon, bombs and later rockets to devastating effect against ground targets, serving in this role until the end of the war in Europe in May 1945.

APPENDICES

Appendix I

Hawker Typhoon IA/B – Early production

The Hawker Typhoon was effectively born out of Air Ministry Specification F.18/37, which called for a monoplane fighter aircraft that would be powered by a new-generation of powerful piston engines in the shape of the Rolls Royce Vulture and the Napier Sabre II. The specifications led to two new fighters from Hawker, the Tornado to be powered by the Vulture and later the Typhoon to be powered by the Sabre.

The first of these new fighters to fly was the Tornado, the prototype of which, P5219, took to the air on 6 October 1939. This aircraft had a top speed approaching 400 mph. Early flight trials revealed problems associated with the airflow around the radiator resulting in same being moved to a position on the forward fuselage below the engine housing, producing the characteristic chin radiator cowl so characteristic of the Typhoon and later Tempest V. The 2nd prototype was redesigned to be built with the chin radiator, this aircraft, which flew for the first time on 5 December 1940, was completed with additional modifications over the first aircraft, including provision to house a new armament of 4 x 20-mm cannon instead of the 12 x 0.303 in machine guns previously specified. The Tornado was soon to be relegated to an experimental status once plans to enter production were abandoned, not least because of the abandonment of production of the of Rolls Royce's Vulture engine.

The second of the two planned fighter designs, the Typhoon, the prototype of which, P5212, conducted its maiden flight on 24 February 1940, was destined to enter operational service. Although wartime urgency produced plans to field the new powerful fighter in summer 1940, these proved to be unrealistic as various problems with the aircraft were ironed out; in particular engine and structural problems. While the first prototype was designed for, and later fitted with an armament of 12 x 0.303 in machine guns, the second prototype, P5216, which flew on 3 May 1941, was designed for an armament of 4 x 20-mm cannon.

Range was in the order of 500 miles, although as with any combat aircraft this depended on aircraft load and operating conditions. The Typhoon had a fuel capacity of 40 gallons in each of the two main tanks and 37 gallons in each of the two nose tanks for a total internal fuel capacity of 154 gallons. Two drop tanks, which could be fitted on the wings, would later allow an additional 90 gallons, 45 in each tank, to be carried. Recommended cruising speed for maximum range to be achieved was 210 mph according to operational documents, although conflicting figures of 254 mph were produced in 1944.

Hawkers produced only 15 production aircraft, the rest being produced by Gloster Aircraft. Typhoon production aircraft developed under specification F.9/40 would eventually extend to 3000+, mostly of the cannon armed MK. IB and IIB, however, the first 110 production aircraft were ordered as Typhoon MK. IA fighters with the originally intended armament of 12 x 0.303 in machine guns – 6 in each wing. The first of these production aircraft, R7576, produced by Glosters, conducted its maiden flight on 27 May 1941. The RAF began receiving Typhoon IA's from August and the first Squadron, No.56, commenced conversion to the type in September that year. The Typhoon IA and IB fighters in service with the Duxford Wing in August 1942 were a mixture of aircraft from the first and second production batches amended to 250 aircraft each.

The Typhoon was developed alongside the Hawker Tornado powered by a Vulture X engine to Specification F.18/37. The prototype of the later, P5219, flew in October 1939. MAP

Climb rate measured on Typhoon R7700 at a weight of 11,070 lb armed with 4 x 20-mm cannon:

Altitude	Climb rate
6,300 ft	2,790 ft per minute
17,800 ft	2,000 ft per minute

Max true level speed in M.S. supercharger: 376 mph at 8,500 ft
Max true level speed in F.S. supercharger: 394 mph at 20,200 ft

Later testing with Typhoon IB R8762 showed a climb rate of 3,840 ft per minute at an altitude of 1,700 ft, dropping to 2,740 ft per minute at 14,300 ft. Testing with this aircraft showed a maximum true level air speed of 357 mph at 1,000 ft, 376 mph at 5,400 ft and 390 mph at 17,200 ft.

Manufacturer's flight testing with Typhoon IA R8198 in late 1941 produced a maximum speed of 405 mph at 22,000 ft.

Typhoon IB Climbing – Speeds for maximum rate of climb:

Up to 16,000 feet	185 mph IAS
At 21,000 feet	170 mph IAS
At 26,000 feet	155 mph IAS
At 31,000 feet	140 mph IAS

For intermediate heights speed is reduced by 3 mph per 1,000 feet.

The 5th production Typhoon IA, R7580 operating with the Air Fighting Development Unit before going to No.56 Squadron. RAF

The following is taken from the Air Ministry Typhoon F. I(B) performance card dated 27.6.44. **Note:** Although there are some differences, the card represents the Typhoon IB in service in 1942. Figures for bomb and rocket carriage have been omitted as they were not pertinent to the aircraft operating in summer 1942.

WEIGHTS
Maximum lb.	11,400
Mean lb.	10,600
Light lb. oil	9,800
	(no fuel bombs or ammunition)
Tare lb.	8,800

DIMENSIONS
Span ft	41.5
Gross wing area sq. ft.	278
Length ft.	32
Height ft. (Tail-down)	15
Crew	1

PERFORMANCE
Take-off over 50 ft. (Max wt.) yards	740
Landing over 50 ft. (Light wt.) yards	870
Service ceiling (Max wt.) ft.	33,000
Service ceiling (Mean wt.) ft.	34,000
Maximum speed M. (mean wt.) mph	374
S. (mean wt.) mph	405

CRUISING SPEED
At 15,000 ft. Most economical mph	254
At maximum weak mixture power mph	330
Time to 15,000 ft. (max wt.) mins	6.2

Performance figures denote an aircraft without bombs or drop tanks.

1 Napier Sabre engine (max) b.h.p.	M. 2,180 (Seal Level)
	S. 1,830 (11,500 ft)

ARMAMENT - GUNS
Bore	20 mm
No.	4 (two in each wing)
Rounds per gun	140

Appendix II

Typhoons involved in Operation Jubilee

R7589, R7595, R7627, R7633, R7645, R7648 , R7649, R7652, R7653, R7672, R7677, R7679, R7680, R7681, R7686, R7687, R7690, R7698, R7702, R7706, R7708, R7711, R7713, R7714, R7715, R7739, R7752, R7823, R7845, R7846, R7847, R7849, R7854, R7855, R7813, R7814, R7815, R7819, R7821, R7822, R7825, R7854, R7961, R8200 and R8221

Despite its early problems the Typhoon went on to become a successful low-level interceptor and fighter bomber. This later production Typhoon IB, DN406, was in service with No.609 Squadron in May 1943. Note the identification markings, which went some way to solving the miss-identification problem that plagued the first Typhoon Squadrons with tragic consequences. RAF

Appendix III

Focke Wulf FW.190

The Focke Wulf FW.190 was a radial engine fighter which entered service with the Luftwaffe in autumn 1941. On the Channel front, the RAF found that even its best fighter, the Supermarine Spitfire V, was outclassed by the new German fighter. The prototype of the FW.190 flew on 1 June 1939, and the first production model to enter operational service, the FW.190A-1, began appearing in Luftwaffe Fighter units of Jagdgeschwader 26 (JG 26), with 6/JG 26 at Le Bourget, Paris, receiving A-1's from August 1941. Early encounters with the new fighter by Spitfire V's of Fighter Command led to the conclusion that the new German fighter was faster and more maneuverable than the British fighter. In overall performance it was superior to the Spitfire V in most respects, one of the few exceptions being the British fighter's better turning performance. Other units eventually received the new fighter which equipped much of the Luftwaffe day fighter force in France by August 1942, with progressively more capable variants entering service. In August 1942 the FW.190A-3 was the main variant in service with JG 26 and JG 2. The A-3 was armed with two fast firing MG 151/20 20-mm cannon outboard of the wing roots and 2 MG 17 machine guns in the engine cowling with provision of two additional machine guns in outer wings.

Air Ministry figures for an FW.190A-3 with a BMW 801D engine tested at the RAE (Royal Aircraft Establishment) were 375 mph (supercharged) at 18,000 ft.

Armament of FW.190A-3: two 7.92 mm machine guns fitted ahead of the cockpit above the engine, a pair of Mauser 20-mm cannon, fitted in the wing roots, one each wing and a pair of Oerlikon type 20-mm cannon housed further outboard on the wings, one each wing. The fuselage mounted machine guns and the wing root cannons were fired through the propeller disc; the machine guns being mechanically synchronized and the cannon being electronically synchronized. The RAE tests concluded that the armament of the German aircraft was superior to the standard armament of any Allied single engine fighter.

WEIGHT: 8,550 lb
WINGSPAN: 34.5 ft
Maximum level speeds – 3 minute rating.

Height ft	T.A.S M.P.H.	R.P.M.	Boost lb/sq.in	Remarks
S.L.	304	2450	4.5	
4,500	326	2450	4.5	
8,000	315	2450	2.4	
11,000	325	2450	4.5	
18,000	375	2450	4.5	
25,000	351	2450	0.5	

RAE tests showed the aircraft to have a rate of climb of 2,760 ft per minute between 0 and 4,000 feet and 2,750 ft per minute at 10,000 – 17,000 feet, dropping to 1,900 at 25,000 ft.

When it appeared on the Channel Front in late summer 1941 the FW.190 showed its superiority over the RAF's premier fighter, the Spitfire VB. USAF

This FW.190A-3 from 11 JG-2 landed in the United Kingdom by mistake after the pilot got lost in June 1942. The aircraft was then test flown at the RAE where its superiority over the Spitfire V was clearly evident. Spitfire IX and some Typhoon pilots were sent to observe the aircraft prior to the Dieppe operation. RAF

Dornier Do.217

The Dornier 217 was a twin-engine medium bomber developed from the same companies Do.17. This aircraft, which equipped units of KG.II in August 1942, was the main threat to the shipping involved in the landings at Dieppe, and therefore, were the main targets for allied fighters including the Typhoons of the Duxford Wing.

GLOSSARY

A/C	Aircraft
CGC	Cine Gun Camera
DFC	Distinguished Flying Cross
Do.	Dornier
DSO	Distinguished Service Order
E/A	Enemy Aircraft
F/Lt	Flight Lieutenant
F/O	Flying Officer
ft	feet
FW	Focke Wulf
HEI	High Explosive Incendiary
HM	His Majesty's
HQ	Headquarters
I	1
IAS	Indicated Air Speed
ib	pound (weight)
II	2
in	inch
IO	Intelligence Officer
IX	9
Mins	minuets
mm	millimeter
MPH	Miles Per Hour
No.	Number
P/O	Pilot Officer
R/T	Radio Transmitter
RAE	Royal Aircraft Establishment
RAF	Royal Air Force
RN	Royal Navy
RPM	Revolutions Per Minute
S/L	Sea Level (also used in some documents as Squadron Leader)
S/Ldr.	Squadron Leader
sq	Square
Sqn	Squadron
Sqdn	Squadron
TAS	True Air Speed
US	United States
USAAF	United States Army Air Force
W/C	Wing Commander
W/Cmdr.	Wing Commander
yds	Yards

BIBLIOGRAPHY

No.56 Squadron Operations Record Book Form 540 Summary of Events August 1942

No.56 Squadron Operations Record Book Form 541 Record of Events August 1942

No.266 Squadron Operations Record Book Form 540 Summary of Events August 1942

No.266 Squadron Operations Record Book Form 541 Record of Events August 1942

No.609 Squadron Operations Record Book Form 540 Summary of Events August 1942

No.609 Squadron Operations Record Book Form 541 Record of Events August 1942

Intelligence Form F, Duxford, Typhoon Wing, Operation Jubilee

Typhoon Aircraft, Tactical Policy document 1942

Individual Combat Reports No.266 and 609 Squadrons

Royal Air Force 1939-45 Official History Volume II

Royal Navy 1939-45 Official History Volume II

W.P. (42) 368 Naval Military and Air Situation 13-20 August 1942

Army Air Forces Material Command Report on Typhoon I

Aeroplane and Armament Experimental Establishment Bascombe Down, Typhoon IB R7700 Climb and level speed performance

Aeroplane and Armament Experimental Establishment Bascombe Down, Typhoon IB R8762 Climb and level speed

Hawker Aircraft Limited Flight Test Reports on Typhoon R8198, R8199 and R7577

Air Ministry and Ministry of Aircraft Production report on performance of captured FW.190A-3, British serial MP499

In addition many other miscellaneous records were used in the research of this volume

ABOUT THE AUTHOR

Hugh, a historian and Author, has published in excess of thirty books; non-fiction and fiction, writing under his own name as well as utilising two different pseudonyms. He has also written for several international magazines, while his work has been used as reference for many other projects ranging from the aviation industry, international news corporations, film media to encyclopedias and the computer gaming industry. He currently resides in his native Scotland

Other titles by the Author include

Hurricane IIB Combat Log – 151 Wing RAF North Russia 1941
Defiant I Combat Log – Fighter Command May-September 1940
RAF Meteor Jet Fighters in World War II, An Operational Log
Eurofighter Typhoon – Storm over Europe
Tornado F.2/F.3 Air Defence Variant
British Battlecruisers of World War 1 – Operational Log, July 1914-June 1915
Boeing X-36 – Tailless Agility Flight Research Aircraft
X-32 – The Boeing Joint Strike Fighter
X-35 – Progenitor to the F-35 Lightning II
X-45 Uninhabited Combat Air Vehicle
F-84 Thunderjet – Republic Thunder
USAF Jet Powered Fighters – XP-59-F-85
XF-92 – Convairs Arrow
The Battle Cruiser Fleet at Jutland
Light Battlecruisers and the 2nd Battle of Heligoland Bight
Spitfire XII Combat Log
Hurricane I Combat Log – France 1940
Spitfire XIV Combat Log
Saab Gripen, the Nordic Myth
Dassault Rafale – The Gallic Squall
F/A-18E/F Super Hornet